Flower Arranging with Garden Flowers

MINEKE KURPERSHOEK

REBO
PRODUCTIONS

© 1997 Rebo Productions b.v., Lisse, the Netherlands
1999 Published by Rebo Productions Ltd.

original title: Bloemschikken uit eigen tuin
text: Mineke Kurpershoek
cover design: Ton Wienbelt, The Hague, The Netherlands
picture editing: Marieke Uiterwijk
editing: Jacqueline Wouda
layout: Signia, Winschoten, The Netherlands
translation: Euro Business Translations, Bilthoven, The Netherlands
typesetting: Hof&Land Typografie, Maarssen, The Netherlands

editing, production and overall co-ordination:
TextCase Boekproducties, Groningen, The Netherlands

Printed and bound in Slovenija

ISBN 1 84053 009 X

Contents

Introduction

Looking around florists' shops and flower stalls these days, I am increasingly struck by the extent to which –as far as cut flowers are concerned– the seasons seem to be becoming irrelevant. You can buy sunflowers in winter and tulips in August. Many of these cut flowers are grown under glass in tropical countries. Cut flowers from all over the world are flown in daily to the huge flower auctions in Aalsmeer, Holland, and then flown out again to buyers in numerous countries. It can be fun to put a big bunch of sunflowers on the table at Christmas, but I have to say that I prefer to see the flowers that bloom in the spring in this country decorating the house at that time of the year, and summer flowers used in profusion in great bouquets in their own season. Obviously there have been gradual changes over the years and I do occasionally have roses on the table in the depths of winter.

In this book I have tried as far as possible to follow the seasons: daffodils and tulips in spring, delphiniums and marguerites in summer, because arrangements of seasonal flowers have a charm all their own. What's more the various materials that go into them are cheaper! In this book I also aim to give you some ideas about flowers, twigs and berries that you can cut from your own garden or from a roadside verge, because you can make a bunch of flowers from the florist even more attractive if you add some wild elements.

This book is divided into four seasons, plus a guide to making flower arrangements and a separate chapter on dried flowers. In the first four chapters I discuss the arrangements that can be created in each season. Each chapter ends with a list of the most commonly-grown flowers, berries, seed pods and foliage that you can gather from your own garden to augment an arrangement.

This section is followed by a chapter devoted to arranging dried flowers. In chapter 6, step-by-step photographs illustrate various techniques for creating some very special flower arrangements. And finally we look at the various materials that are available for use in flower arranging.

Flower stall

Left: an arrangement created after a painting by an old master, containing a wealth of bulbs and summer flowers.

CHAPTER I

The joys of spring
(March-April-May)

There is probably no time of year that we look forward to so eagerly as the spring. We greet every bulb that thrusts its head out of the soil with delight, and watch as the buds on trees and shrubs open into the brightest of green leaves. When the first shrubs, bulbs and perennials start to flower, the insect life wakes up and chubby bumble bees buzz from flower to flower.

A cheerful arrangement in yellow including the parrot tulip 'Texas Gold', ranunculus, arum lilies and shrubby hare's ear (Bupleurum)-all secured in a piece of florist's foam wedged in the neck of the vase only.

Simple but charming: the white flowers of Amelanchier *and birch catkins in a misty blue jug.*

The earliest of the flowers-snowdrops, winter aconites, violets, primroses and lungwort-have very short stems and so are best suited for an arrangement in something like a milk jug, a small mug or a tiny vase. A couple of branches of *Cornus* or flowering dogwood and the false hazel *Corylopsis,* or perhaps birch or alder catkins, can be placed with them in a separate vase. If you then add a couple of interesting objects, such as a little figurine or a few photograph frames, you will find you have created a charming still life. Catkins contain a great deal of pollen which will fall as a gentle haze around the arrangement. The effect is very subtle-but do bear in mind that this pollen can stain tablecloths or rugs.

As spring progresses, more and more flowers appear in the garden. There are more materials to choose from and the options for producing an

The trailing stems of asparagus fern and grasses turn this simple bunch of tulips in a tall vase into a charmingly airy arrangement.

Not really a proper flower arrangement, but a delightful still life with early spring flowers like crocuses and violets. The glass holds a Christmas rose (Helleborus orientalis), a lovely plant that blooms in the garden very early in the year.

A simple bowl of daffodils.

attractive arrangement increase, if only because the stalks of the flowers that bloom later in the season are longer. The first peonies come out at the end of May and there are irises in all sorts of wonderful shades.

An exuberant spring arrangement incorporating a variety of daffodils, with Forsythia, Amelanchier (serviceberry) and Ribes (flowering currant). Leaving the piece of florist's foam in which the flowers are arranged protruding well above the neck of the vase makes it appear that the daffodils have very long stems. Do remember to top up the water in the vase at least once a day, otherwise the top of the foam will dry out.

T I P

Always arrange branches and twigs taken from shrubs in tepid water containing special cut flower food for shrubs. It makes it much easier for them to take up water.

When a large arrangement starts to look tired, any flowers that are still good can be used to make a simple posy.

Detail of a delicate arrangement of white ranunculus and greenish-white guelder rose (Viburnum opulus 'Roseum'). Commercial growers bring this shrub into flower under glass and twigs can often be bought very early in the year. In the garden, guelder rose blooms in May and June.

An arrangement from the garden. Grape hyacinths (Muscari), lungwort (Pulmonaria) and the seed heads of pasqueflowers (Pulsatilla), framed by ivy leaves (Hedera helix).

An attractive arrangement of unusual ranunculus, exotic kangaroo paw (Anigozanthos) and waxflower (Chamelaucium). The unusual border of curved leaves sets it off perfectly.

A simple but effective design using a few magnolia twigs and the purple flowers of the winter heliotrope (Petasites hybridus). Butcher's broom (Ruscus) leaves conceal the lead pin-holder used to secure the arrangement.

An artless jugful of snakes-head fritillaries (Fritillaria meleagris).

Narcissi and hyacinths arranged in a loose tangle of plastic-coated chicken wire, which has been concealed beneath wisps of straw. The addition of a few coloured eggs turns this into a delightful arrangement for Easter.

Right: start with the Butcher's broom (Ruscus) foliage, and then add the tulips, the star-of-Bethlehem (Ornithogalum umbellatum) and a few catkins. All the materials have short stems, so they can be placed in the vase without support.

TIP

Arrange Christmas roses and other members of the hellebore family in water with cut flower food at half strength.

An arrangement in warm tones. Roses, ranunculus, antirrhinums, Peruvian lilies (Alstroemeria) and shrubby hare's ear Bupleurum.

Yellow with a touch of white: the colours of a sunny spring. The terracotta container was lined with a piece of tough plastic and then two well-soaked chunks of florist's foam were wedged into it.

Above: you can create a delightful still life by grouping together containers of different shapes and sizes but made from the same material. Fill the vases with little bunches of flowers-each one different.

A charming arrangement in a simple basket. A nest of foliage holds a selection of flowers in shades of pink and white, enlivened by just a few splashes of yellow.

It can be as simple as this. Grasses contrasting with the dark leaves of the copper beech (Fagus sylvatica 'Purpurea').

Below: the curving stems of Solomon's seal (Polygonatum) fan out elegantly above the compact cluster formed by the green and white tulips (Tulipa viridiflora 'Greenland', bishop's lace (Ammi Majus) and a bunch of green grapes. You will always need something to hold an arrangement in a shallow container. Florist's foam is the best choice.

Following pages: *the addition of campion seed pods (Silene dioica) and seed heads of honesty (Lunaria annua) that are just changing colour gives this arrangement a very individual touch.*

A shallow container with a large lead pin-holder provides a firm base for this simple arrangement of rhododendron flowers surrounding a mass of Spanish bluebells (Hyacinthoides hispanica, syn. Scilla hispanica).

TIP

Leave daffodils and narcissi in water on their own for 24 hours before you arrange them with other flowers. Don't cut the stems again, because the slimy sap that oozes out can affect the other flowers.

Flowers with hairy stems, including sweet peas (lathyrus), *are best arranged in only a little water. If the water is too deep, it can work its way up through the hairs and cause the flower to rot. Do take care that all the flowers always have the ends of their stalks in water.*

A wildflower bouquet of native British bluebells (Hyacinthoides non-scripta, syn. Scilla non-scripta), campion (Silene dioica), three-cornered leeks (Allium triquetrum) and fern fronds.

Right: a simple yet stunning arrangement using the parrot tulip 'Estella Rijnveld' and a few stems of bleeding heart (Dicentra spectabilis). The tulips lying on the table can be kept fresh for longer by placing each stem individually in a plastic flower holder filled with water and sealed with a rubber cap (see page 131).

Below: detail of a bouquet of tulips, roses, lilac, sweet peas, birch catkins and asparagus fern.

An old resin pot with a piece of florist's foam holds an arrangement of double tulips, sweet peas, sea lavender (Limonium) and a few twigs of Eucalyptus. The foam has been covered with moss. A simple arrangement with a charm all its own.

TIP

It is easy to encourage branches of early-flowering shrubs into bloom. Bring them indoors and let them acclimatize before you take them into the warmth of the living room.

Below: a bunch of double late peony-flowered tulips set off quite simply with an assortment of foliage-young red Photinia leaves, fennel (Foeniculum) and snowberry (Symphoricarpos). Inside the basket is a container holding a tangle of plastic-coated chicken wire to support the arrangement.

Common broom (Cytisus scoparius), *yellow archangel* (Lamium galeobdolon) *and* Pachysandra *leaves create a simple bouquet arranged in a glass tank. Make sure that there are as few leaves as possible actually in the water. This looks much more attractive and it also means that bacteria have less opportunity to contaminate the water.*

Left: a long, shallow container is ideal for an arrangement of clumps; a substantial clump of buttercups on the left, a bunch of irises in the middle and yellow archangel on the right. The spaces between them are filled with flowering grasses. A few tufts of lawn grass give the arrangement an extra fillip, and emphasize its countryside character. You can make it even more attractive by placing the container on something like a baking sheet and covering the sheet entirely with tufts of grass.

Below: a still life in white, green and blue. The white tulips and grasses are arranged in an old white jug with a blue pattern. In front of this is a white bowl with a blue rim, filled with the same white tulips and grasses plus golden feverfew (Tanacetum parthenium) and bishop's lace (Ammi majus). The addition of a few bright blue delphiniums sets off the blue in the jug and bowl.

Above: detail of an arrangement incorporating arum lilies (Zantedeschia), golden feverfew (Tanacetum parthenium), Peruvian lilies (Alstroemeria) and ranunculus.

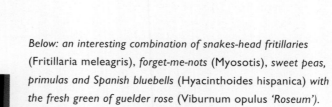

Below: an interesting combination of snakes-head fritillaries (Fritillaria meleagris), forget-me-nots (Myosotis), sweet peas, primulas and Spanish bluebells (Hyacinthoides hispanica) with the fresh green of guelder rose (Viburnum opulus 'Roseum'). The deep blue glass vase holding the flowers and the other vases around it give the arrangement added impact.

Above: two moss-covered containers hold a generous clump of variegated sage (Salvia officinalis 'Tricolor') and a group of lilies-of-the-valley (Convallaria majalis). A piece of string has been tied around the container of sage to hold twigs of rosemary (Rosmarinus officinalis) in place. *The moss covering the container of lilies-of-the-valley is secured with a strong tendril of ivy.*

A cloud of Queen Anne's lace (Anthriscus sylvestris).

Left: spring shades into summer: tulips, peonies, Queen Anne's lace (Anthriscus sylvestris) and white dead nettle (Lamium album).

The blue, mauve and lilac shades of dame's violet (Hesperis matronalis), sweet peas, Spanish bluebells (Hyacinthoides hispanica) and Eustoma show to great effect against the large zinc tubs. The arrangement also incorporates Solomon's seal (Polygonatum).

Below: flowering quince or japonica (Chaenomeles).

This arrangement of variegated gardener's garters (Phalaris arundinacea 'Picta'), young shoots of wormwood (Artemisia ludoviciana), a couple of large Telekia leaves, a few limes and some clumps of lilies-of-the-valley illustrates just how effective a combination of greens with just a touch of white can be. The whole thing sits in a block of plastic-wrapped florist's foam wedged into a basket.

Previous pages: a simple arrangement of bugle (Ajuga), some grasses and young leaves taken from a variegated Hosta.

Right: another charming arrangement in green and white. White ranunculus and sweet peas are set off by the green of the guelder rose (Viburnum opulus 'Roseum') and the seed heads of stinking hellebore (Helleborus foetidus). The bright green is a type of asparagus fern, the grey-green foliage is Eucalyptus.

From your own garden

Trees and shrubs
azalea *(Rhododendron)*
broom *(Cytisus)*
catkins, alder *(Alnus)*, birch *(Betula)*, hazel *(Corylus)* and willow *(Salix)*
Corylopsis
crab apple *(Malus)*
Deutzia
Enkianthus
flowering currant *(Ribes)*
flowering quince or japonica *(Chaenomeles)*
Forsythia
heather *(Erica)*
ivy *(Hedera)*
Laburnum
Magnolia
ornamental cherry *(Prunus)*

Pieris
Rhododendron
serviceberry *(Amelanchier)*
Skimmia
Spiraea arguta
Stachyurus
sweet gale or bog myrtle *(Myrica)*
viburnum, including guelder rose *(Viburnum opulus* 'Roseum')
Weigela
witch hazel *(Hamamelis)*

Jacob's ladder (Polemonium caeruleum) *has white or blue flowers depending on the cultivar. The yellow leaf is the golden-leafed variety of mock orange* (Philadelphus coronarius 'Aureus').

Deutzia

Globeflower (Trollius europaeus 'Goliath')

Yellow columbine (Aquilegia chrysantha *'Yellow Queen'*)

Perennials
alkanet *(Anchusa)*
Aster tongolensis
bearded iris *(Iris germanica)*
bleeding heart, Dutchman's breeches *(Dicentra)*
Brunnera
Christmas rose and stinking hellebore *(Helleborus)*
columbine *(Aquilegia)*
elephant's ear *(Bergenia)*
foam flower *(Tiarella)*
globeflower *(Trollius)*
Jacob's ladder *(Polemonium)*
leopard's bane *(Doronicum)*
lily of-the-valley *(Convallaria)*
lungwort *(Pulmonaria)*
pasqueflower *(Pulsatilla)*
peony *(Paeonia)*
periwinkle *(Vinca)*
Phlox divaricata
primrose *(Primula)*
Queen Anne's lace *(Anthriscus)*

Solomon's seal *(Polygonatum)*
spurge *(Euphorbia)*
violet *(Viola)*
wood spurge *(Euphorbia amygdaloides)*

above: leopard's bane (Doronicum orientale)

right: bearded iris (Iris germanica *'Bianca') come in a great many colours and shades; there are also bicoloured varieties.*

wood spurge (Euphorbia amygdaloides)

Bulbs

crown imperial *(Fritillaria imperialis)*
daffodil *(Narcissus)*
Dutch iris *(Iris hollandica)*
grape hyacinth *(Muscari)*
hyacinth *(Hyacinthus)*
ornamental onion *(Allium cowanii* and *Allium neapolitanum)*
snakes-head fritillary *(Fritillaria meleagris)*
Spanish bluebell, bluebell *(Hyacinthoides,* syn. *Scilla)*
star-of-Bethlehem *(Ornithogalum)*
tulip *(Tulipa)*

Left: Christmas rose (Helleborus orientalis)

Below left: Spanish bluebell (Hyacinthoides hispanica, *syn.* Scilla hispanica)

Below: the parrot tulip 'Blue Parrot' among blue and white forget-me-nots (Myosotis).

Annuals and biennials

dame's violet, sweet rocket *(Hesperis matronalis)*
forget-me-not *(Myosotis)*
foxglove *(Digitalis)*
honesty *(Lunaria)*
pansy *(Viola)*, pink *(Dianthus)*
wallflower *(Erysimum cheiri)*

Below: universal pansies in an old manger are a flower arrangement in themselves.

Peony (Paeonia japonica 'Marie Brand')

Below: the stately foxgloves (Digitalis purpurea) form a backdrop to one of the most attractive of the ornamental onions (Allium christophii).

CHAPTER 2

The height of summer
(June-July-August)

The selection of cut flowers, foliage and grasses available in the summer is so wide that you can easily arrange a display in a different colour or with an entirely different structure every single week. At this time of the year flowers are relatively inexpensive since commercial growers can grow them outside rather than in costly heated glasshouses. This is the season for creating wonderful arrangements using flowers from your own garden-perhaps augmented with materials collected from roadside verges or meadows, or with a bunch of flowers bought from the florist's or flower stall.

A cheerful arrangement of Iceland poppies (Papaver nudicaule) with a few stems of lady's mantle (Alchemilla). The flowers are held in a ball of chicken wire.

Pick the flowers as early in the day as possible, before the sun gets too hot and the moisture in flowers and stems has had time to evaporate. When you set out to pick wild flowers, always take a container of water with you in the car or your bicycle basket so that you can put the materials you gather in water straight away. If you intend to pick flowers in the wild, you must be aware of which species are protected-some are close to extinction and picking them not only despoils the environment, it is also against the law. You can pick things like Queen Anne's lace (or cow parsley), most grasses, sorrel and butter-cups with impunity, but do bear in mind that wild flowers are often less robust than their culti-vated cousins and may well be host to an array of wild life in the form of aphids, whitefly and so on. If they are, display your arrangement of wild flowers on the garden table so that you can still enjoy them.

You can sometimes buy sweet peas in large sprays complete with flowers, leaves and fine tendrils. This makes for a very striking and unusual arrangement which requires little in the way of additional material. A few short twigs of lilac blossom from the garden anchor the arrangement. Give the lilac a thorough drink of lukewarm water to which you have added cut flower food for flowering shrubs before you arrange the blooms in florist's foam.

Left: flowers do not always have to predominate. Here we have a delightful still life with just a single stem of Queen Anne's lace (Anthriscus).

Below: an old-fashioned posy. The rose in the centre is surround-ed by a frill of small flowers and leaves, all framed in a border of larger leaves.

The addition of various grasses, picked from the roadside verge, and some lady's mantle (Alchemilla mollis) turns an ordinary bunch of roses into an enchanting arrangement.

Right: this arrangement of green tones shows what can be accomplished with only a few materials. Two large lead pin-holders have been placed some distance apart in a shallow glass dish, with just a couple of iris leaves pushed into each one. A few vivid green amaranthus tassels (Amaranthus caudatus 'Viridis') and some petty spurge (Euphorbia peplus) picked in the wild have been added to the holder at the back. The duckweed floating on the water gives the arrangement an unusual touch. The white stones conceal the pin-holders. If you wanted to turn this into a still life, you could place a few larger pebbles alongside it, or perhaps add some small glass dishes containing just a little duckweed.

Columbines (Aquilegia) *and a roadside grass create an airy arrangement finished with a frame of young leaves of the leopard plant* (Ligularia dentata). *The white stones conceal the pin-holder in which the materials are arranged.*

Below: Allium christophii, *lady's mantle* (Alchemilla mollis), *greater masterwort* (Astrantia major 'Rubra'), *a late peony* (Paeonia) *and grasses arranged in plastic-coated chicken wire concealed in a low bowl. The foliage is butcher's broom* (Ruscus).

Below: roadside treasures. Comfrey (Symphytum), *camomile* (Matricaria), *shepherd's purse seeds* (Capsella bursa-pastoris), *white dead nettle* (Lamium album), *Queen Anne's lace* (Anthriscus sylvestris), *grasses and coltsfoot foliage* (Tussilago farfara) *are the ingredients of this arrangement.*

Right: it's always nice to make a bunch of flowers go a bit further. Here we have an arrangement both in the ewer and in the accompanying bowl. The flowers are bistort (Polygonum bistorta), thistle (Circium japonicum 'Rose Beauty') and Phlox paniculata. The arrangement in the bowl is held in florist's foam.

Following pages: a truly delightful arrangement in an old zinc can. The can had a hole in it, so it was lined with a piece of plastic sheeting and a piece of well-soaked florist's foam was wedged into it to hold the arrangement of gentians (Gentiana makinoi 'Royal Blue'), love-in-a-mist (Nigella), amaranthus or love-lies-bleeding (Amaranthus hypochondriacus), caper spurge (Euphorbia lathyris) and petty spurge (Euphorbia peplus) picked in the wild.

Shop-bought roses and phlox set off by the pale pink spikes of bistort (Polygonum bistorta syn. Persicaria bistorta) and Veronica spicata from the garden. The arrangement was created in florist's foam after the flowers had been given a good long drink of water.

Daisies flower in the border as well as along the roadside. They have been arranged in this old-fashioned jug with comfrey (Symphytum), camomile (Matricaria) and Queen Anne's lace (Anthriscus sylvestris). The dark brown spikes of great pond sedge (Carex riparia) spark up this predominantly white arrangement.

Below: many of the herbs, like this borage (Borago officinalis), have lovely flowers. Here it is arranged in a charming display with cornflowers (Centaurea cyanus) and chervil (Anthriscus cerefolium).

Its casual feel adds to the charm of this arrangement. Arum (or calla) lilies (Zantedeschia) with guelder rose (Viburnum opulus 'Roseum') and a few stems of the magnificent tall spurge (Euphorbia characias ssp. wulfenii).

Further proof that an arrangement does not have to be complicated. A bunch of chive flowers (Allium schoenoprasum) is simply surrounded by a frame of grey-green hosta leaves.

This yellow and white arrangement has been supported in florist's foam, but plastic-coated chicken wire is equally effective. This arrangement incorporates a white cultivar of the annual Lavatera trimestris, arum (or calla) lilies (Zantedeschia), lady's mantle (Alchemilla mollis), foxgloves (Digitalis), hosta leaves, fern fronds and foliage from the fine-leaved butcher's broom (Ruscus).

Below: an arrangement in a shallow dish of water with a few flowers floating on the surface is easy to create and extremely effective. This charming arrangement is composed of just three roses and three lavatera blooms, with the tiny flowers of masterwort (Astrantia) and lady's mantle (Alchemilla mollis), floating between them. The attractive foliage also comes from the lady's mantle.

Below: a trough has been used to create a linear arrangement. In this style of flower arranging, most of the flowers and any foliage is arranged vertically. The individual materials are grouped together: in this case the delphiniums as the highest elements, and next to them the woolly grey leaves of lamb's ears (Stachys byzantina), the grey-leaved stems sold as Kochia and, at a lower level, blue scabious (Scabiosa caucasia) and fleabane (Erigeron). The dark foliage comes from the copper beech (Fagus sylvatica 'Purpurea') and the slightly lighter leaves come from a rex begonia.

A simple cake is given a festive touch by placing a small bouquet of sweet peas in pastel shades in the centre.

Left: a garden party usually calls for large, eye-catching arrangements. It is much better to use one really striking display than several small ones, which can often get lost among the guests. This display, arranged in a large garden vase containing florist's foam, includes foxgloves, peonies, delphiniums and roses. The use of plenty of foliage shows off the individual blooms to best effect. Using foliage from the garden also keeps down the cost of an arrangement like this.

Right: a large arrangement of roadside and hedgerow plants. The huge leaves in the background are butterbur (Petasites hybridus).

TIP

Alliums will last for a long time in water, but the water often starts to smell very unpleasant after only a few days, particularly in a warm room. It is a good idea to change the water every four or five days.

A low bowl arrangement always looks good and is fairly easy to create. Turn the bowl regularly while you are arranging the materials to ensure that you get a good balance of flowers and that the arrangement is symmetrical. The flowers used here are arum or calla lilies (Zantedeschia), milfoil (Achillea), lady's mantle (Alchemilla mollis) and Saint John's wort (Hypericum perforatum) picked in the wild. Alchemilla and Pachysandra leaves provide the finishing touch.

This display in a gravy boat is arranged in florist's foam. The floral elements are scabious (Scabiosa), bellflowers (Campanula lactiflora), masterwort (Astrantia) and sage (Salvia officinalis). The grey-green foliage is lavender, and the heart-shaped leaves are wild ginger (Asarum caudatum).

TIP

When you pick lilac blossom from your own garden, make sure that some of the tiny florets are already open. Remove some of the leaves from the stem and stand the branches in water at about 15°C (60°F) to which you have added cut flower food for shrubs.

By picking just one or two specimens of all the different flowers in your garden you can create a cheerful mixed arrangement. You can have a lovely display like this without leaving gaps in your borders.

For an elegant centrepiece, why not make an arrangement in a serving dish or sauce boat from the dinner service you will be using. This display of Geum coccineum 'Borisii' and orange spurge (Euphorbia griffithii 'Fireglow') is arranged in florist's foam.

A low bowl of cranesbill (Geranium himalayense), delphiniums, candytuft (Iberis amara) and cornflowers (Centaurea cyanus) arranged in an old dish with a pattern that echoes the colours of the flowers.

Arranging a low, symmetrical display in a container with a foot lends it style and elegance. The effect is reinforced by the curving flower stems and the lovely fern fronds. The arrangement also contains the annual Lavatera, *bishop's lace (*Ammi majus) *and golden feverfew (*Tanacetum parthenium).

*A glass bowl on a foot holds a wealth of garden flowers: monkshood (*Aconitum), *the round-headed leek (*Allium sphaerocephalon), Phlox paniculata *and love-in-a-mist (*Nigella), *whose fine, feathery leaves create an airy effect.*

A real summer display of the annual Lavatera trimestris, *tall verbena (*Verbena bonariensis), *monkshood (*Aconitum) *and baby's breath (*Gypsophila). *The grasses soften the edges of this arrangement.*

*Another wonderful collection from the wild. Tansy (*Tanacetum vulgare), *wild parsnip (*Pastinaca sativa), *wild carrot (*Daucus carota), *sorrel (*Rumex) *and grasses have been arranged in a glass tank.*

A magnificent combination of blues shading to purple in this arrangement of delphiniums, veronica, sweet peas, stonecrop (Sedum spectabile) and the cultivated form of Eustoma.

Right: the best way to arrange an attractive, round display in a wide container is to use a loose tangle of chicken wire to hold the flowers, although you can place them straight into the container. This arrangement includes bishop's lace (Ammi majus), lavender blue and white scabious (Scabiosa caucasia), delphiniums, poppies (Papaver orientale), phlox and sage (Salvia officinalis). The fern fronds and grasses complement the bishop's lace in giving this compact arrangement an airy feel.

Although the flowers in this arrangement-roses, silkweed (Asclepias tuberosa) and the orange rudbeckias (Echinacea purpurea)-could equally well have come out of the garden, they were in fact bought from a flower stall, as were the ivy and the grey-green Eucalyptus foliage.

TIP

The seed heads of shepherd's purse are wonderful in arrangements, either fresh or dried. They are extremely useful materials that can simply be picked in the wild.

The first berries start to appear on the shrubs towards the end of the summer. The snowberry (Symphoricarpos albus) is not a particularly attractive shrub, but the pink or white berries are highly decorative. Combined with phlox and the lovely yellow green umbels of dill (Anethum graveolens), they make a charming centrepiece for the table.

From the garden

Trees and shrubs
beech *(Fagus)*
broom *(Cytisus)*
butterfly bush *(Buddleja)*
California lilac *(Ceanothus)*
Clematis
crab apple *(Malus)*
Fuchsia
guelder rose *(Viburnum opulus* 'Roseum' *)*
honeysuckle *(Lonicera)*
Hypericum
Kalmia
Kolkwitzia
lavender *(Lavandula)*
lilac *(Syringa)*
mock orange *(Philadelphus)*
ornamental cherry *(Prunus)*
privet *(Ligustrum)*
rose
smoke bush *(Cotinus)*
snowberry *(Symphoricarpos)*
Spiraea, various species and cultivars
tamarisk *(Tamarix)*
whitebeam *(Sorbus)*

The sorrel (Rumex), tansy (Tanacetum vulgare), evening primroses (Oenothera biennis), toadflax (Linaria vulgaris) and even the sunflowers (Helianthus annuus) in this arrangement were gathered in the wild.

The green-flowered tobacco plant (Nicotiana 'Lime Green') *makes this a really striking arrangement. It has been combined with marguerites* (Argyranthemum frutescens, syn. Chrysanthemum frutescens), *bishop's lace* (Ammi majus) *and the double golden feverfew* (Tanacetum parthenium 'Goldball'). *You can grow all these plants in your own garden.*

Perennials

African lily *(Agapanthus)*
alkanet *(Anchusa)*
Anthemis
aster
Astilbe
avens *(Geum)*
Baptisia australis
bellflower *(Campanula)*, several varieties
bergamot *(Monarda)*
bistort *(Polygonum bistorta* syn. *Persicaria bistorta)*
blanket flower *(Gaillardia)*
blazing star *(Liatris)*
bugbane *(Cimicifuga)*
buttercup *(Ranunculus aconitifolius)*
carnation *(Dianthus)*
catchfly *(Lychnis chalcedonia)*
catnip *(Nepeta)*
columbine *(Aquilegia)*
coneflower *(Rudbeckia)*
coral bells *(Heuchera)*
cranesbill *(Geranium)*
Crocosmia
cupid's dart *(Catananche)*

Delphinium
Echinacea
Eupatorium
evening primrose *(Oenothera)*
fleabane *(Erigeron)*
gentian *(Gentiana)*
giant hyssop *(Agastache)*
globe thistle *(Echinops)*
gyp, baby's breath *(Gypsophila)*
Heliopsis
horned pansy *(viola cornuta)*
Hosta, foliage
Inula
knapweed *(Centaurea macrophylla)*
lady's mantle *(Alchemilla)*
lamb's ears *(Stachys byzantina)*
leopard plant *(Ligularia dentata)*
London pride *(Saxifraga urbium)*
loosestrife *(Lysimachia)*
loosestrife *(Lythrum)*
lupin *(Lupinus)*
mallow *(Malva)*
marguerite *(Leucanthemum)*
marjoram *(Origanum)*
masterwort *(Astrantia)*
meadow rue *(Thalictrum)*

This display of wild flowers includes milfoil (Achillea millefolium), *camomile* (Matricaria), *the seed heads of Queen Anne's lace* (Anthriscus sylvestris) *and sorrel* (Rumex). *A large lead pin-holder was placed at the bottom of the container and used to secure the first sturdy stems of Queen Anne's lace and sorrel. This created a criss-cross of stalks in which the other flowers were arranged.*

milfoil *(Achillea)*
monkshood, aconite *(Aconitum)*
obedient plant *(Physostegia)*
oxeye *(Buphthalmum)*
Pachysandra
pearly everlasting *(Anaphalis)*, also good for
    drying
peony *(Paeonia)*
Peruvian lily *(Alstroemeria)*
poppy *(Papaver orientale)*
Potentilla
prairie mallow *(Sidalcea)*
pyrethrum *(Tanacetum coccineum)*
red hot poker *(Kniphofia)*
red valerian *(Centranthus)*
rue *(Ruta graveolens)*
Salvia, species and cultivars
scabious *(Scabiosa)*
sea holly, eryngo *(Eryngium)*
sea lavender, statice *(Limonium)*
silkweed *(Asclepias)*
sneezeweed *(Helenium)*
sneezewort *(Achillea ptarmica)*
soapwort *(Saponaria officinalis)*
spurge *(Euphorbia)*
Stachys grandiflora syn. *S. macrantha*
stonecrop *(Sedum)*
sweet pea *(Lathyrus latifolius)*

A red climbing rose against a background of mock orange
(Philadelphus coronarius).

tall verbena *(Verbena bonariensis)*
tansy *(Tanacetum vulgare)*
Thermopsis
thistle *(Circium)*
thrift, sea pink *(Armeria)*
tickseed *(Coreopsis)*
turtle head *(Chelone)*
Veronica, several varieties
wild ginger *(Asarum)*
wormwood foliage *(Artemisia)*
Yucca

A magnificent clump of deep blue lavender (Lavandula angustifolia 'Hidcote') contrasts with the yellow-green flowers of the common rue (Ruta graveolens) with its fine blue-green leaves. Dogs hate the smell of this evergreen plant, so plant it by your garden gate to deter wandering canines from coming in.

There are several varieties and cultivars of the African lily (Agapanthus). These hardy plants certainly deserve a place in the garden.

The Astilbe *is an attractive border perennial which will be happy in full sun or light shade. The plume-like flower spikes come in white, various shades of pink, and red. The bellflowers (Campanula lactiflora)in the background are equally good as cut flowers.*

The dark red foliage in the background is the smoke bush (Cotinus coggyria 'Royal Purple' or 'Purpureus'). It provides a beautiful foil to the ornamental onions (Allium christophii).

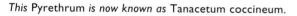

This Pyrethrum *is now known as* Tanacetum coccineum.

A hot border with a whole selection of flowers for cutting-the orange Peruvian lily (Alstroemeria aurea 'Orange King'), flaming red catchfly (Lychnis chalcedonia) and Geum, red roses, rust brown sneezeweed (Helenium), pale yellow lilies (Lilium) and an attractive cultivar of milfoil (Achillea millefolium). The mullein (Verbascum) gives this border an attractive vertical accent.

Bulbs
Allium
anemone *(Anemone coronaria)*
Dahlia
foxtail lily *(Eremurus)*
Freesia
Gladiolus
Ixia
lily *(Lilium)*
Ornithogalum thrysoides and *O. arabicum*
pineapple flower *(Eucomis)*
ranunculus *(Ranunculus asiaticus)*
Triteleia laxa

Annuals and biennials
African marigolds *(Tagetes)*
Amaranthus
bells of Ireland *(Molucella),* also good for drying
bent grass *(Agrostis nebulosa),* also good for drying

bishop's lace *(Ammi majus)*
blanket flower *(Gaillardia pulchella)*
blue lace flower *(Trachymene coerulea* syn. *Didiscus coerulea)*
borage *(Borago)*
Bupleurum griffithii
bush marguerite *(Argyranthemum frutescens)*
candytuft *(Iberis amara)*
Canterbury bell *(Campanula medium)*
Carthamus
chervil *(Anthriscus cerefolium)*
China aster *(Callistephus)*
Chrysanthemum coronarium and *C. segetum*
Clarkia
cockscomb, Prince of Wales' feather *(Celosia)*
coriander *(Coriandrum)*
cornflower *(Centaurea cyanus)*
cosmos *(Cosmea atrosanguineus, C. bipinnatus* and *C. sulphureus)*
crimson clover *(Trifolium incarnatum)*
delphinium *(Delphinium consolida)*
dill *(Anethum graveolens)*
Euphorbia marginata
flossflower *(Ageratum)*
gardener's garters *(Phalaris canariensis),* also good for drying
Godetia grandiflora
golden feverfew *(Tanacetum parthenium)*
Gomphrena, also good for drying
gyp, baby's breath *(Gypsophila elegans)*

Lilium 'Star Gazer'. There is a huge variety of lilies. Their large blooms make such a striking statement in the border that it seems a shame to cut them.

Among the numerous varieties of Euphorbia is the annual E. marginata.

Cosmos (Cosmos bipinnatus) *is an excellent annual for cutting.*

Nasturtiums (Tropaeolum majus), *a bright and cheerful summer flower useful in small arrangements.*

hare's tail grass *(Lagurus ovatus)*, also good for drying
Helichrysum, also good for drying
Helipterum, also good for drying
honesty *(Lunaria annua)*
Iceland poppy *(Papaver nudicaule)*
immortelle *(Xeranthemum)*, also good for drying
Lonas annua, also good for drying
love-in-a-mist *(Nigella)*
lupin *(Lupinus nanus)*
marigold *(Calendula)*
mignonette *(Reseda)*
nasturtium *(Tropaeolum majus)*
opium poppy *(Papaver somniferum)*
pansy *(Viola)*
Penstemon
Phacelia
Phlox drummondii
poppy *(Papaver rhoeas)*
quaking grass *(Briza media)*, also good for drying
Rudbeckia hirta
Salvia farinacea and *Salvia horminum*

scabious *(Scabiosa atropurpurea)*
Senecio bicolor, grey foliage
snapdragon *(Antirrhinum)*
soapwort *(Saponaria)*
spurge *(Euphorbia lathyris)*
statice *(Limonium sinuatum)*, also good for drying
stock *(Matthiola)*
sunflower *(Helianthus annuus)*
sweet william *(Dianthus barbatus)*
sweet pea *(Lathyrus odoratus)*
teasel *(Dipsacus)*
tickseed *(Coreopsis grandiflora)*
tobacco plant *(Nicotiana)*
tree mallow *(Lavatera trimestris)*
Verbena
Zinnia

TIP

All the members of the spurge family (Euphorbiaceae) contain a milky sap in all parts of the plant. This sap is toxic and a skin irritant. When damaged, the plants will 'bleed'. If you gather these flowers from your own garden or cut off the end of the stem from flowers you have bought, you can stop this bleeding by immersing the end of the stem in water at 20°C (68°F) for a minute. Arrange the flowers in water with cut flower food at half strength.

CHAPTER 3

Autumn glory
(September-October-November)

In autumn, until the first frost, there are still plenty of flowers in the border-perennials, annuals and even some bulbs. As well as these late-flowering varieties there are all sorts of shrubs with their branches weighed down by berries or with wonderful autumn leaf coloration. Not all branches with beautifully coloured foliage can be used in displays, however, since the leaves fall at the slightest touch. Some, however, retain their red leaves for a considerable time. One of these is the American oak *(Quercus rubra)* and you can often find branches for sale in the florist's.

In September there are still plenty of flowers in the border for cutting-annuals like cosmos (Cosmea bipinnatus) *and dill* (Anethum graveolens) *and perennials like phlox* (Phlox paniculata) *and turtle head* (Chelone obliqua).

Seeds, seed heads and grasses are still abundant. They can be used in arrangements or dried for later use with other dried flowers. (See chapter 5.)

Gradually everything in the garden dies down, and it is the evergreens that prevent the garden from looking too bare and provide us with enough materials to aid us in our flower arranging during the winter. The only time you should not cut material from your own garden is when the weather is freezing.

At the end of the chapter about winter there is a list of evergreen and semi-evergreen shrubs and perennials.

This arrangement derives its charm from the great contrast between the shapes of the different flowers. It is another of those round displays that are always so effective and yet simple to create. This one contains a few white lavatera blooms, the yellow-flowered oxeye daisy (Buphthalmum), sneezeweed (Helenium), Heliopsis, dill (Anethum graveolens) and the seed heads of gardener's garters (Phalaris canariensis).

TIP

If you want to cut elder branches (Sambucus nigra) to use in an arrangement, do it before the berries are too ripe. If you leave them until they are fully ripe, the berries are likely to drop and can cause nasty stains on whatever surface the container has been placed.

Detail of an unusual arrangement consisting predominantly of foliage. It is the textures and colours that provide the surprising contrasts here. Just a couple of zinnias, a twig of snowberry (Symphoricarpos albus) and the green spikes of the annual Ambrosinia mexicana have been added.

Detail of an arrangement in strongly contrasting colours. The purple anemone (Anemone coronaria 'De Caen') with its black centre stands out against the background of the tiny lilac florets of the Trachelium caeruleum and the yellow flowers of the golden rod (Solidago) and the hybrid Solidaster form. A few asters (Aster pringlei 'Monte Carlo') have also been added to the display.

TIP

Did you know that the edible Jerusalem artichoke (Helianthus tuberosus) is a member of the sunflower family?

Left: an autumn arrangement consisting almost exclusively of ethereal flowers, giving it a very individual character. The tiny, lacy lilac flowers of the statice (Limonium latifolium) define the structure. Between them are a few stems of monkshood (Aconitum), tall verbena seed heads (Verbena bonariensis), the pink spikes of a Spiraea and the small blue eryngo (Eryngium planum). The foliage comes from the arum lily and the plumes of grass are Miscanthus.

This arrangement combines the large leaf of the elephant's ear (Bergenia), *which is just changing colour, the pink umbels of the stonecrop* (Sedum telephium) *and the spikes of* Persicaria amplexicaule *syn.* Polygonum amplexicaule.

True September beauties, these asters (Aster pringlei 'Monte Cassino' *or* Aster pringlei 'Monte Carlo'), *with their long sprays of dainty white flowers. You can grow the former of these two cultivars in your own garden. A few roses, chrysanthemums and hydrangea heads* (Hydrangea macrophylla) *complete the arrangement.*

Left: the elder (Sambucus nigra) *has wonderful green and purple-black berries in autumn. The arrangement was started by placing twigs of elderberries in this slender vase. They provided a framework to hold the loosestrife* (Lythrum salicaria), *which was arranged in the vase to create an open fan shape. A scattering of blackberries and a few common reed spikelets* (Phragmites australis) *add the finishing touch.*

The flowers and berries in this piece are arranged in a container holding a block of florist's foam. By keeping the stems short, you can create an attractive, compact arrangement that would make an ideal table decoration. The berries are Saint John's wort (Hypericum androseanum), the green umbels are the buds of Sedum spectabilis, a garden perennial that will produce pink flowers later in the season. The lovely pink trumpets are Eustoma.

Left: this display has been arranged in a ball of plastic-coated chicken wire. It incorporates the lovely warm golden flowers of the Helianthus, the yellow blooms of the coneflower (Rudbeckia nitida) *—a perennial that can easily grow to a height of two metres (over 6 ft)— a few pale yellow Peruvian lilies* (Alstroemeria) *and double gypsophila* (Gypsophila paniculata 'Bristol Fairy').

Below: this delightful little 'garden', arranged in florist's foam, has been created from a selection of flowers taken from the herbaceous border —orange-red Cape fuchsias (Phygelius capensis), yellow umbels of fennel (Foeniculum vulgare), the seed heads of the butterfly bush (Buddleja davidii), African marigolds (Tagetes tenuifolia) and zinnias.

Above and above left: small yellow chrysanthemums (Dendranthema) and hips from a floribunda rose (Rosa multiflora) have been arranged between mahonia leaves with their wonderful autumn colour (Mahonia aquifolium). A block of florist's foam was used to hold them in place.

A flower arrangement? No, just a magnificent head of
'Romanesco', a lime green variety of the cauliflower.

Below: a block of florist's foam covers the whole of the bottom
of a glass dish with a foot. A smaller dish with a foot, also
containing florist's foam, is placed in the centre. Firstly, short
twigs of the dark-leaved smoke bush (Cotinus coggyria
'Purpureus') were inserted into the foam so that they effectively
concealed it from view. Sprigs of heather (Calluna) and stonecrop (Sedum spectabilis) were then arranged between the
leaves. The individual side shoots of the stonecrop umbels were
used separately since a whole flower head would have been too
big for a small arrangement like this. The addition of a few
sprigs of elderberries around the edges provided the finishing
touch. The weight of the berries causes them to hang elegantly
over the edge.

TIP

*Buy sunflowers when the flowers are well
open. When you get them home, cut a
length off the end of the stems and put
them in lukewarm water containing cut
flower food for herbaceous plants. This is
extremely important if you want them to
last well.*

A lead container supports an arrangement of sunflower stalks
(Helianthus annuus) with the flower heads on top; highly
decorative and very easy to do.

A display of flowers and leaves in colours that look good
together. Perhaps not the peak of the flower arranger's art,
but charming for all that.

These yellowing Hosta *leaves illustrate the fact that even dying foliage can still be used to great effect in a flower arrangement. The size of the leaves means they stand out against the tiny flowers of the golden rod* (Solidago). *The rust-brown flowers of the sneezeweed* (Helenium 'Moerheim Beauty') *and the orange berries spark up the display.*

Below: how to transform a gift into more than just a pretty dish; and it's extremely easy to do.

Easy to create with just a few materials, and yet the effect of this arrangement in the two little dove vases is utterly charming. A piece of florist's foam was placed in the back of each dove. This was used to hold a few columbine leaves (Aquilegia), *just changing colour, the fluffy flowers of hare's foot clover* (Trifolium arvense), *picked in the wild, a few musk mallow flowers* (Malva moschata), *wild marjoram* (Origanum vulgare) *and a seed head.*

An interesting still life with a very unusual arrangement in one of the containers. A piece of florist's foam was placed in the container and used to hold a clump of lavender stalks and several groups of grasses in the centre. The pleated and partly rolled-up leaf of the butterbur (Petasites hybridus) was pushed in around the edge. If you then knot and plait the grasses very loosely, you will have created a very different arrangement with very few materials.

This wreath was made during a holiday in France, where all the materials were found in the woods or along the sides of the road. They include the prickly seed cases of the sweet chestnut (Castanea sativa), acorns (Quercus), fern fronds, oak leaves and columbine foliage (Aquilegia), a beautiful grey lichen, the seed heads of the wild carrot (Daucus carota) and the flower spikes of the horsemint (Mentha longifolia). The photograph below shows a detail of the wreath.

Previous pages: a block of florist's foam was positioned on one of the long sides of this large basket. In this case it was placed on a small tray, but you could also wrap it in cling film. The arrangement has been deliberately placed to one side, so that the shape of this magnificent basket can still be seen. The first step was to insert the long brambles (Rubus fruticosus) with their beautiful autumn colours into the florist's foam. They give the arrangement length and, because they have been arranged to the front, add a jaunty touch. The second element was the bunch of rose hips (Rosa multiflora), followed by the fluffy seed heads of old man's beard (Clematis vitalba), the hydrangeas, a few tendrils of ivy and, in the centre, some brown medlars (Mespilus germanica). The basket handle must not be allowed to be a dividing line between the individual materials, but should go through the arrangement. This is achieved by arranging a few of the stems on either side of the handle.

Right: keep your eyes peeled whenever you go for a walk, because almost all the materials you see can be used. This bamboo-pattern vase holds a few short twigs of sea buckthorn (Hippophae rhamnoides), with a couple of common reed stalks (Phragmites) to add height, and a single trailing bramble (Rubus fruticosus) with the leaves just turning red.

Below: an old enamel ring mould from grandma's kitchen is the basis of this simple arrangement. Small pieces of florist's foam were pushed into the ring and then filled with short-stemmed flowers and berries. They include Michaelmas daisies, snowberries (Symphoricarpos albus), alder cones (Alnus glutinosa) and the black berries of the dogwood cornel (Cornus sanguinea).

The hydrangeas (Hydrangea macrophylla), *the black privet*
berries (Ligustrum vulgare) *and the red Skimmia buds came*
from the garden, the roses were bought. Imagination and a few
bits and pieces from the garden can transform an ordinary
bunch of flowers into something quite special.

A gift decorated with a tuft of lichen moss and a tiny sprig of
cowberry (Vaccinium vitis-idaea).

Left: this arrangement was created on a special bouquet
holder. They can be used to make an arrangement for a
funeral, but are also ideal for creating a display to hang
on a wall or door for a festive occasion. Yellow chrysanthe-
mums (Dendranthema), *orange* Euphorbia fulgens,
Peruvian lilies (Alstroemeria) *and yellow snapdragons*
(Antirrhinum majus) *have been arranged among the*
grey Eucalyptus *foliage.*

The large, shiny leaves of elephant's ear (Bergenia) make this arrangement of Michaelmas daisies and privet berries (Ligustrum vulgare) something more than just a bunch of flowers. They also add volume to the display. The pendent sprays of white snowberries (Symphoricarpos albus) add sparkle.

Below: a small posy of hydrangeas (Hydrangea macrophylla), a few roses and the metallic blue berries of Viburnum tinus with a border of salal leaves (Gaultheria shallon). Some florists have taken to wrapping a bouquet like this in paper that they roll down all round the top edge, creating a charming frame for the posy.

This compact little arrangement is easy to create with all sorts of flowers from the garden. When you visit someone, an arrangement like this is a much more personal gift than a bunch of flowers from the florist. It also means that your hostess can put it straight on to the table and devote her attention to her guests because she does not have to go looking for a suitable vase, or find a bucket to stand the flowers in for the time being.

Left: a lovely decoration for the garden table: a garden urn filled with gourds and green peppers.

Below: the large display was made for a special occasion. The big basket conceals a bucket holding a large block of florist's foam in which the bouquet of chrysanthemums (Dendranthema), snowberries (Symphoricarpos albus) and Eucalyptus has been arranged.

With autumn in full swing, the displays can be very different from spring and summer arrangements. This is what makes using seasonal materials so much fun. A tall, flattened cone of florist's foam is secured to a copper nut dish. It stays in place because it is fixed to the base with waterproof tape (see page 137). The first elements to go in are the blue-green rue leaves (Ruta graveolens), *and the bunches of crab apples (Malus),* and the tiny rosehips of Rosa multiflora *are then inserted* between them. Make sure that enough leaves and fruits hang over the edge of the dish —first and foremost to conceal the tape, but also because it makes the arrangement much more elegant. Check that there is always enough water in the container and mist the display regularly to prevent it from drying out.

A magnificent autumn arrangement incorporating berries, apples and even pine cones. A few flowers from the border nestle in a luxuriant background of hop flowers (Humulus lupulus) with the violet berries of the beauty berry (Callicarpa bodinieri var. giraldii), teasels (Dipsacus fullonum), hydrangeas (Hydrangea macrophylla) and the seed heads of the opium poppy (Papaver somniferum).

A display of chrysanthemums (Dendranthema), the red berries of the Cotoneaster and the leaves of the serviceberry (Amelanchier) in their wonderful autumn colours –all arranged in a large basket.

The seed pods revealing the red berries of stinking gladwin (Iris foetidus) have been arranged against a green background of the leaves and early fruits of the ivy (Hedera), Ruscus and Skimmia.

Right: this unusual and striking display is arranged in florist's foam. The orange seed heads of the Chinese lantern (Physalis alkekengi var. franchetii) were wired first because the individual stems were too short. They do not have to be kept in water since they can also be used in dried form. A double wreath of ivy leaves was then pushed into the foam around the lanterns, followed by the curved stems and seed pods of Crocosmia crocosmiiflora). The bunches of elderberries (Sambucus nigra) were added last.

A double border of large ivy leaves has been arranged in florist's foam in a shallow dish. The leaves are lying flat on the rim of the dish. Seed heads of the yellow water flag (Iris pseudacorus) and crab apples (Malus) were then added in the centre. The wreath used to frame the arrangement is made from long, dried tendrils of goose grass (Galium aparine), gathered in the wild.

Right: tremendous impact for very little work-you just have to come up with the idea. A large pumpkin in a bed of hop flowers (Humulus lupulus).

A block of florist's foam has been positioned against the side of a flat copper dish. It is held in place by a plastic pin holder that has been attached to the bottom with adhesive tape. The various materials are arranged more or less in groups. The longest twigs of firethorn (Pyracantha) are pushed horizontally into the foam first, followed by the fruit of the flowering quince (Chaenomeles), and the bunches of black privet berries (Ligustrum vulgare) go opposite this. The variegated leaf is Leucothoë fontanesiana 'Rainbow', the blue- green foliage is rue (Ruta graveolens).

Chrysanthemums (the new name is Dendranthema), *are on sale all year round but they should actually bloom in the autumn. This simple arrangement is held in florist's foam pushed into a small metal cake tin. The arrangement also includes white snowberries* (Symphoricarpos albus), *a few small sprigs of* Euphorbia fulgens *and grey* Eucalyptus *foliage.*

A sauce boat containing nothing but a few beautifully coloured brambles (Rubus fruticosus). The lovely coloration in the leaves came about because the bush was growing in very poor, gritty soil exposed to full sun. The arrangement is secured in florist's foam.

A lovely wreath of cowberry (Vaccinium vitis-idaea) *fastened with thin string to a circle of strong wire.*

Fruit and nuts are arranged on a bed of mulberry (Morus) and Viburnum leaves in the basket in the centre of this table decoration. The basket is surrounded by a wreath of mulberry and viburnum leaves (which can if necessary be attached to the table cloth with transparent adhesive tape). The fragrant fruit of the japonica or flowering quince (Chaenomeles) are placed on the leaves, singly or in groups, more or less evenly spaced. The gaps are then filled with nuts —in this case sweet chestnuts (Castanea sativa) and hazel nuts (Corylus avellana). On each plate there is a mulberry leaf on which the guest's name has been written in felt tip pen.

Below: this wreath was made from the leaves of the fern Polypodium vulgare during a holiday in Finland, and photo-graphed against a background of lichen.

Himalayan honeysuckle (Leycesteria formosa)

A strawberry punnet, lined with plastic sheeting on which a block of florist's foam has been placed, is the base for this arrangement. The materials used are red roses, ivy berries, red berries from the hawthorn (Crataegus monogyna), a few twigs of yew (Taxus) and grasses from the roadside verge.

Below: Hydrangea paniculata

A very unusual arrangement. Numerous clumps of a variety of grass were placed in a tall glass vase. The tips of the clumps were bound together with thin copper wire. Weighting the ends of the grass clumps made them bend over elegantly. They were weighted by hooking a tiny apple or a cluster of berries to the copper wire or by attaching a glory lily (Gloriosa) to the tip. The glory lily can be placed in a flower holder or the end of the stem can be wrapped in a piece of wet cotton wool with gutta-percha tape around it to prevent it from drying out. These materials are concealed by a dry leaf secured with copper wire. The red patches on the grasses are from an autumn leaf.

Below: the seed heads of old man's beard (Clematis vitalba).

T I P

Yew (Taxus) *makes a magnificent hedge or, if it is not clipped, tall shrubs or trees. Take care if there are children about because the black seeds inside the red fruits are poisonous. Cattle have died after eating these seeds or yew branches.*

Hydrangea
ivy *(Hedera)*
Mahonia
roses
Saint John's wort *(Hypericum)*
salal *(Gaultheria shallon)*
smoke tree *(Cotinus coggyria)*
snowberry *(Symphoricarpos albus)*

From the garden

Trees, shrubs and climbers
Clematis, various varieties
Fuchsia
heath *(Erica)*
heather *(Calluna)*
Hibiscus
Himalayan honeysuckle *(Leycesteria formosa)*
Hydrangea paniculata

Left: the blue seed pods of Decaisnea fargesii

Below: the bramble or blackberry (Rubus fruticosus)

Bramble leaves turn wonderful colours in autumn if the plant is growing in poor soil.

Trees, shrubs and climbers with berries, hips, haws and fruit

If you want to plant one of the shrubs listed below so that you can harvest berries from it for flower arranging, ask the grower which species or cultivar is the best. Also find out whether the plant is female and if it will set fruit without a male specimen nearby. If it won't, you will have to plant a male plant alongside the berry-bearing female.

alder *(Alnus)*, alder cones
Aronia
Aucuba
beech *(Fagus sylvatica)*, beech nuts
Berberis
bittersweet *(Celastrus)*
bladder nut *(Staphylea)*
bladder senna *(Colutea)*

The fruit of the flowering quince (Chaenomeles) *has a delicious fragrance.*

blueberry *(Vaccinium myrtillus)*
bramble, blackberry *(Rubus)*
butterfly bush *(Buddleja)*
Callicarpa
Clerodendrum
conifers, cones from various species
Cotoneaster

Saint John's wort berries (Hypericum androseanum).

The lovely fruit of the crab apple (Malus 'Prof. Sprenger').

old man's beard *(Clematis vitalba)*
Pernettya
pine *(Pinus)*, pine cones
privet *(Ligustrum)*
rose *(Rosa), rose hips*
rowan *(Sorbus)*
Saint John's wort *(Hypericum)*
sea buckthorn *(Hippophae)*
serviceberry *(Amelanchier)*
Skimmia
snowberry *(Symphoricarpos albus)*
Spiraea
Stranvaesia
sweet chestnut *(Castanea sativa)*
Viburnum
whitebeam *(Sorbus aria)*

These prickly cases conceal the edible fruits of the sweet chestnut (Castanea sativa).

cowberry *(Vaccinium vitis-idaea)*
crab apple *(Malus)*
Decaisnea fargesii
dogwood *(Cornus)*, various species
elder *(Sambucus)*
Euonymus
firethorn *(Pyracantha)*
flowering cherry *(Prunus)*, several varieties
flowering currant *(Ribes)*
flowering quince, japonica *(Chaenomeles)*
hawthorn *(Crataegus)*
hazel *(Corylus)*, hazelnuts
Himalayan honeysuckle *(Leycesteria)*
holly *(Ilex)*
hop *(Humulus lupulus)*, hop flowers
horse chestnut *(Hippocastanum)*
ivy *(Hedera)*
Liquidambar
medlar *(Mespilus)*
oak *(Quercus), acorns*

Perennials

Anemone
Arum italicum, berries
Aster pringlei
bugbane *(Cimicifuga)*
Chinese lantern *(Physalis),* seed heads
chrysanthemum *(Dendranthema)*
coneflower *(Rudbeckia)*
Crocosmia crocosmiiflora, seeds
elephant's ear *(Bergenia),* foliage
eryngo, sea holly *(Eryngium)*
Eupatorium
giant hyssop *(Agastache)*
golden rod *(Solidago)*
gooseneck loosestrife *(Lysimachia clethroides)*
Heliopsis
Liriope
loosestrife *(Lythrum)*
meadow rue *(Thalictrum)*
Michaelmas daisy *(Aster)*
monkshood, aconite *(Aconitum)*
obedient plant *(Physostegia)*
oxeye daisy *(Buphthalmum)*

Persicaria amplexicaule *syn.* Polygonum amplexicaule
Phlox
red hot poker *(Kniphofia)*
sneezeweed *(Helenium)*
Solidaster
statice *(Limonium)*
stonecrop *(Sedum)*
sunflower *(Helianthus)*
tickseed *(Coreopsis)*
Trachelium caeruleum
Tricyrtis
turtle head *(Chelone)*
yellow water flag *(Iris pseudacorus),* seed heads

Bulbs

Several of the bulbs, corms and tubers will produce flowers until the first frost.

Cyclamen hederifolium
Dahlia
Members of the onion family producing seed

After flowering, the arum (Arum italicum) produces attractive heads of green berries which then turn orange.

giant hyssop (Agastache foeniculum)

Dahlia 'Tally Ho'

heads for drying include *Allium aflatunense*, *A. christophii, A. schubertii*

Annuals

Plants generally regarded as annuals, but which can be kept in a light, frost-free place, will bloom until the first night frost. They include pelargoniums.

For drying

There are many flowers that lend themselves to drying. They include immortelles and the 'everlasting' *Helichrysum*, various grasses and seed heads. We look at the drying of other flowers and twigs in chapter 5.

Perennials with seed heads and flowers that are easy to dry

cardoon *(Cynara)*
carline thistle *(Carlina)*
Chinese lantern *(Physalis)*
cupid's dart *(Catananche)*
eryngo, sea holly *(Eryngium)*
everlasting flower *(Helichrysum)*
globe thistle *(Echinops)*
grasses
Gypsophila
lavender *(Lavandula)*
ornamental grasses, various species
ostrich fern *(Matteuccia)*
pearly everlasting *(Anaphalis)*
statice *(Goniolimon* and *Limonium)*
stonecrop *(Sedum telephium)*
yarrow *(Achillea filipendula)*

Annuals and biennials with seed heads and flowers that are easy to dry

Ammobium
bells of Ireland *(Molucella)*
Carthamus
gardener's garters *(Phalaris canariensis)*
Gomphrena
Helichrysum
Helipterum
honesty *(Lunaria)*
immortelle *(Xeranthemum)*
Lonas
love-in-a-mist *(Nigella)*
love-lies-bleeding *(Amaranthus)*
maize, sweetcorn *(Zea mays)*
opium poppy *(Papaver somniferum)*
ornamental gourd *(Cucurbita)*
ornamental grasses, various species
poppy *(Papaver)*
scabious *(Scabiosa prolifera* and *S. stellata)*
shoo fly plant *(Nicandra)*
statice *(Limonium)*
teasel *(Dipsacus)*

Phlox paniculata

CHAPTER 4

Winter contrasts
(December-January-February)

In the winter months, we are largely reliant for cut flowers on the range grown by commercial growers under glass. In the introduction to this book, I said that when designing the arrangements I would, as far as possible, use the flowers growing in our gardens at the relevant time of the year.

This does not, of course, apply to the winter months-roses, chrysanthemums and carnations, after all, are summer and autumn plants. We don't have to take it quite that literally.

In this period too, we look forward to the spring with its many bulbs and shrubs-like guelder rose and lilac-that can be brought into flower early in the year.

We can do this ourselves-bring branches of shrubs into the house where they will soon come into flower. *Forsythia* and the flowering currant *(Ribes)* are good examples.

Hydrangeas (Hydrangea macrophylla) *turn the most wonderful colours in autumn and become even more striking after there has been a light night frost. Cut them when the flowers feel leathery and either arrange them in a vase or hang them up to dry. In this arrangement they have been incorporated with ivy leaves* (Hedera helix) *and brambles* (Rubus fruticosus). *The dark red, glossy berries of the hawthorn* (Crataegus monogyna) *liven up the display.*

The low, wide-weave basket has been lined with a piece of plastic on which has been placed a block of well-soaked florist's foam. Make sure that the block protrudes at least two centimetres (about an inch) above the edge so that sprigs can also be pushed into the sides to create a flowing line with elegantly drooping leaves and berries. Start with the foliage elements, in this case ivy (Hedera), Eucalyptus and Pachysandra and arrange the other materials between them —berries from the ivy and the Eucalyptus, and yellow holly berries (Ilex aquifolium 'Amber' is a good variety). Finish off with a few chrysanthemums (Dendranthema) and the dried fruits of Leucadendron plumosum, which you will need to wire.

Pieces of florist's foam cut to fit have been wedged into these two individual tart tins and a small oval candle has been placed on top of each. Tiny sprigs of Eucalyptus have been arranged around the candles, followed by the individual blooms of a white cultivar of the daisy-flowered chrysanthemum (Dendranthema) and the snowberry (Symphoricarpos albus). If you put a whole group of these tiny arrangements together on a silver salver, you will have created a delightful table decoration.

Left: a shallow glass bowl has been lined with bun moss (Grimmia pulvinata). Start by placing the moss on the bottom and then work your way a ring at a time up the sides. Lay a few red peppers or some shiny Christmas baubles in it and you have an unusual Christmas decoration.

You won't need much in the way of materials to make a Christmas decoration like this, but it does take quite a bit of time to do (see page 125).

Here a ball of florist's foam, wrapped in sphagnum moss to make it firmer, has been secured to a glass candlestick. The candle was placed in the centre and the various materials were then pushed into the ball. Tufts of the delicate flowers of the pearly everlasting (Anaphalis triplinervis), dried and wired, and wired red-brown pecan nuts were arranged between small sprigs of holly (Ilex).

Making a wreath like this one does call for a bit of experience. However you can buy wreaths of pine or larch cones ready made, and then add your own decorations-immortelles perhaps, like the ones in the photograph, or tiny Christmas baubles which you can attach with a glue gun.

At Christmas we go all out in the kitchen and we put more effort into decorating the table. A flower arrangement is surely a must. For this occasion we have found a pretty glass vase on a foot. The red, white and green materials —appropriate colours for a Christmas decoration— are arranged in florist's foam. Start by arranging a base of ivy leaves and berries. Then space the white roses evenly over this green background. The red berries of the holly (Ilex aquifolium) and the floribunda rose (Rosa multiflora) give the display that Christmassy feel. Fill in with flower spikes of gardener's garters (Phalaris canariensis) and the trailing stems of periwinkle (Vinca minor).

In December, Christmas is an important factor in creating flower arrangements and all sorts of other decorations.

The first few months of the year are the time for bulbs-tulips, narcissi, daffodils, hyacinths, anemones, snowdrops and grape hyacinths. If the weather is mild, some very early bulbs will already be in flower.

There are also shrubs that flower in the winter. If we want to create an arrangement out of materials from the garden at this time of year it will generally be a simple one, since it is a shame to pick too many of the scarce flowers that brighten up the winter scene.

Early-flowering bulbs and perennials are adapted to severe cold and will soon wilt in the warmth of the house.

They will last a far shorter time than the flowers outside in the wind and rain. The Christmas rose, for example, will flower for many months in the garden, but we can consider ourselves lucky if it survives for much more than a week indoors.

The lists at the end of this chapter include bushes and shrubs that have attractively coloured or unusually shaped branches. There is also a list of evergreens. Obviously this group of plants and shrubs lends itself to use all year round, but in other seasons of the year there are so many other-deciduous-shrubs that this group is not as important then.

This wreath has been bound on to a strong metal frame using reel wire (see page 137). Small sprigs of the blue spruce (Picea pungens 'Glauca'), red holly berries (Ilex aquifolium), larch cones (Larix) and pine cones (Pinus) have been alternated around the base.

The different materials have been arranged on a moss wreath-a quick and easy way to achieve an effect.

Detail of the wreath on the left.

An opulent table decoration photographed in a stately home. Notice the long garland draped on the table and echoed along the mantlepiece. Garlands like this are wound around a piece of cord or a length of metal wire (see page 127).

Below: pushing cloves into an orange creates a highly decorative, deliciously scented ball. The more cloves you use, the longer the oranges will keep. Arrange them on a dish with a few sprigs of holly and perhaps some Christmas baubles and ribbons.

T I P

Never take bun moss or sphagnum moss from the wild. Always buy it from the florist or garden centre.

Detail of the table decoration above left. The basis of the arrangement is a cone of florist's foam with sphagnum moss secured around it.

Right: of course there has to be a Christmas tree too. Although it's not a flower arrangement, decorating it calls for some of the same skills.

A group of flowering plants can also create the effect of a flower arrangement. Poinsettias (Euphorbia pulcherrima), azaleas and calamondins (x Citrofortunella microcarpa) are closely grouped on a magnificent table.

This 'orange mountain' was constructed around a core of wet florist's foam surrounded by moss. The oranges were stacked up first and then sprigs of holly leaves and bunches of orange firethorn berries (Pyracantha) were pushed into the foam. The oranges were held in place with the aid of wooden skewers. Oranges have also been used as candlesticks. The candles and the holly were simply pushed straight into the whole orange. If you prefer, you can use the peel of half an orange. Put a piece of florist's foam in it and push the candle and the holly into the foam.

Below: a less elaborate arrangement is equally appropriate in December. If you want to give it a Christmassy touch, add a few pine cones or shiny glass baubles on wires. A piece of florist's foam has been placed in a plastic-lined basket. Arranged in it are Skimmia twigs with foliage and flowers in bud, heather (Calluna), black privet berries (Ligustrum vulgare) and the grey-leaved branches of an exotic plant sold as kochia.

An arrangement of daffodils, cornelian cherry (Cornus mas) and foliage from Elaeagnus ebbingei, an attractive evergreen shrub with leaves that are silver on the underside.

Below: springs creeps gradually closer and there are plenty of flowers from the spring-flowering bulbs to buy to help us get into the mood. A lead pin-holder in a glass vase holds twigs of the evergreen Mahonia aquifolium. The narcissi and the twigs of sweet gale or bog myrtle (Myrica gale) were then positioned in this sturdy base. The stones at the bottom of the vase conceal the pin-holder.

After the excitement of Christmas it's time to calm down again, and this can be reflected in our flower arrangements. A few stems of Chamelaucium uncinatum in white or pink, with just a couple of ivy leaves, create a charming effect.

Next pages: anemones can be bought all winter long, even though they only flower in the garden in summer. This lovely flower, Anemone coronaria, with its dark heart, comes in a great many colours and shades. They have been arranged here in a low vase containing a block of florist's foam. The foliage is butcher's broom (Ruscus hypophyllum).

Hyacinths (Hyacinthus orientalis) *have thick, soft stems and are consequently difficult to arrange in florist's foam. It is easier simply to put them in a vase or use a very loose tangle of chicken wire to hold them. If you do want to put them in foam, poke a hole in the foam first with a pencil or stick and then put the hyacinth in. A general rule of thumb in flower arranging is to create a background of foliage, and then put the flowers in place. In the case of hyacinths, however, because of their difficult stems it is easier to start with the hyacinths and then add the foliage, the roses and the ivy with their thinner, stronger stalks.*

Below: the soft orange of these Tulipa 'Apricot Beauty' makes a wonderful contrast with the grey-green of the Eucalyptus. The twigs arranged between them are sweet gale or bog myrtle (Myrica gale), a plant that grows in wet heaths and fens mainly in the north of the British Isles.

Nuts mounted on wire are often available in the shops at Christmas time. However, you can wire nuts yourself by drilling a tiny hole in the nut with a very fine drill and pushing in a sturdy stub wire.

A dish containing a selection of floating flower heads from the glorious Christmas rose (Helleborus).

Willows form fluffy catkins early in the year and the coltsfoot (Tussilago farfara) is one of the earliest perennials to bloom in the wild. Here, a lead pin-holder has been placed in a glass tank, and the willow twigs (Salix) have been pushed into it. A layer of white stones in the bottom of the container conceals the pin-holder, and a couple of clumps of coltsfoot have been positioned on the stones.

A piece arranged in a lead pin-holder placed in the bottom of a shallow dish. The birch twig was wedged securely, followed by the snowdrops (Galanthus) and the grape hyacinths (Muscari). If these tiny flowers with their thin stalks won't stay upright in the pin-holder, use raffia to tie them together in small bunches. The spray of ivy and a couple of sprigs of heather were arranged almost horizontally to break up the hard line of the edge of the dish. Here, a tuft of grass and a few stones have been used to hide the pin-holder.

Tulips often need no other materials to set them off.

One way of showing off the individual blooms.

Below: the long efflorescences of Garrya elliptica.

Below: there are already plenty of catkins in late winter —these come from the hazel (Corylus avellana).

A large display of amaryllis needs a fairly wide vase because of the thickness of the stems. Here they have been arranged with the magnificent green-white guelder rose (Viburnum opulus 'Roseum') and a very decorative type of Eucalyptus with graceful, willow-like foliage.

From the garden

Trees and shrubs

Chimonanthus praecox
cornelian cherry *(Cornus mas)*
Garrya elliptica
hazel *(Corylus avellana)*
heath *(Erica)*
heather *(Calluna)*
Hydrangea
Mahonia
Prunus subhirtella 'Autumnalis'
Sarcococca humilis
sweet gale, bog myrtle *(Myrica gale)*
Viburnum bodnantense 'Dawn'
willow *(Salix)*
winter jasmine *(Jasminum nudiflorum)*
witch hazel *(Hamamelis)*

The witch hazel (Hamamelis mollis) *is a slow-growing shrub.*

Below: *holly berries are always identified with Christmas decorations. This is the variegated* Ilex altaclerensis *'Lawsoniana'.*

winter jasmine *(Jasminum nudiflorum)*

TIP

The amaryllis is a bulb that will not tolerate cold; the temperature must not be allowed to drop below 15°C (60°F). The stems of these giant flowers are hollow and very thick, and often have to support a great many very large blooms. It is by no means unusual for the stems to buckle under the weight. Reinforce them by pushing a thin cane through the stalk very carefully until it is just under the flower head. Another problem with amaryllis stems is that they often split at the bottom. You can prevent this by binding the bottom part of the stem with raffia or thread.

Evergreen shrubs with foliage and cones that can be used in flower arrangements in the winter months

Aucuba

box *(Buxus)*

cherry laurel *(Prunus laurocerasus* and *P. lusitanica)*

conifers, branches and cones of various species

Cotoneaster, several varieties

Elaeagnus ebbingei and *E. pungens*

Enkianthus

Euonymus fortunei and *Euonymus japonicus*

Fatsia japonica

holly *(Ilex)*

ivy *(Hedera)*

Ledum groenlandicum

Leucothoë walteri 'Rainbow'

Lonicera nitida and *L. pileata*

The dainty, delicate snowdrop (Galanthus)

Mahonia

Osmanthus

Pachysandra

periwinkle *(Vinca minor* and *V. major)*

Photinia x fraseri 'Red Robin'

Pieris

privet *(Ligustrum ovalifolium* and *L. vulgare* 'Atrovirens')

Rhododendron, various species

rue *(Ruta graveolens)*

salal *(Gaultheria shallon)*

Sarcococca

Senecio greyi

Skimmia

Viburnum, various species

The black and green berries of the female ivy (Hedera helix). The shrub form (Hedera helix 'Arborescens') has the same type of flowers and berries as the species.

Shrubs with interesting colours or unusual growth habits

contorted willow *(Salix matsudana* 'Tortuosa')

contorted hazel *(Corylus avellana* 'Contorta')

dogwood *(Cornus stolonifera* 'Flaviramea' and *C. stolonifera* 'Kesselringii')

red-barked dogwood *(Cornus alba* 'Sibirica' and *C. alba* 'Bloodgood')

Salix udensis 'Sekka'

Salix alba 'Dart's Snake'

Perennials

Christmas rose *(Helleborus)*

elephant's ears *(Bergenia),* foliage

Bulbs

daffodil *(Narcissus)*

snowdrop *(Galanthus)*

TIP

There are various types of cut flower food, including cut flower food for bulbs. Make sure that you add the right amount of water to the contents of the sachet. Always top up the vase with water containing the right concentration of cut flower food.

CHAPTER 5

Dried flowers

Strawflowers or immortelles are flowers that feel dry and papery, like straw, at an early stage. These flowers can simply be hung upside in small bunches and used in dried flower arrangements as soon as the stems are hard.

This little basket is filled with the white flowers of Helichrysum vestitum, *the glossy buds of the blue strawflower* (Catananche caerulea), *bay leaves* (Laurus nobilis), *statice* (Limonium tataricum), *larch cones and some fake fruit as a fun touch.*

The range of true strawflowers is not that great. The best known are:

Ammobium alatum
blue strawflower *(Catananche caerulea)*
Gomphrena globosa, white, pink, red, mauve, yellow and orange depending on the cultivar
Helichrysum cassianum, pink
Helichrysum subufolium, yellow
Helipterum manglesii (syn. *Rhodante manglesii),* white and pink
immortelle *(Helipterum humboldtianum),* syn. *H. sanfordii),* yellow
paper flower *(Xeranthemum annuum),* white and pink
rat's tail statice *(Limonium suworowii* syn. *Psylliostachys suworowii),* pink
statice *(Limonium sinuatum* syn *Statice sinuata),* in various shades
strawflower *(Helichrysum bracteatum),* in various shades except mauve and blue

Helipterum manglesii

Miss Willmott's ghost (Eryngium giganteum)

Teasel (Dipsacus fullonum)

Greater quaking grass (Briza maxima)

Various thistles, both annuals and perennials, grasses and, of course, the old-fashioned Chinese lantern *(Physalis alkekengi franchetti)* and honesty *(Lunaria annua)* –which used to grace parlour mantlepieces combined with corn cobs and feathers in dusty displays– can also be used in dried flower arrangements. Gypsophila, particularly the double-flowered cultivars of *Gypsophila paniculata*, is easy to dry, as is the yellow annual *Lonas inodora* and the likewise yellow achillea *(Achillea filipendula).*

Over the years a great many other annuals and perennial flowers have been added to this range. Most of them have been subjected to a hot air treatment for a fairly short period in a huge shed. You can easily dry these flowers yourself.

Air drying

You can find flowers and seed heads suitable for drying by this method in the garden, in roadside verges and on waste ground. It is very important to pick the flowers when they are dry, because if there is any moisture between the petals the flowers will soon rot. After you have picked them, you remove some or all of the leaves. Make them into bunches –not too many stems in each bunch– and hang them up somewhere that is preferably warm and in any event dry and dark. By keeping the size of the bunches relatively small and not hanging them too close together you can reduce the risk of rotting. Heat and air circulation are important factors. It is a good idea to secure the bunches firmly with an elastic band since the stems will shrink during the drying process.

You can achieve good results if you use this method on the strawflowers, grasses and thistles listed above (see also chapter 3). Other flowers suited to this method of drying are:

Acanthus
achillea
Allium
Astilbe
Astrantia
Ballota
bells of Ireland *(Molucella)*
bergamot *(Monarda)*
Carthamus
catnip *(Nepeta)*
cockscomb, Prince of Wales' feather *(Celosia)*
cotton lavender *(Santolina)*
Dahlia
Delphinium

dill *(Anethum graveolens)* and other umbelliferous plants
golden rod *(Solidago)*
Hydrangea
Kochia
lady's mantle *(Alchemilla)*
lamb's ears *(Stachys byzantina)*
lavender *(Lavandula)*
Liatris
love-in-a-mist *(Nigella)*
love-lies-bleeding *(Amaranthus)*
marigold *(Calendula)*
marjoram, oregano *(Origanum)*
meadow rue *(Thalictrum)*
mimosa
pearly everlasting *(Anaphalis)*
Phlomis
rosemary *(Rosmarinus)*
sage *(Salvia)*
sea lavender or statice *(Limonium)*

Chinese lantern (Physalis alkekengi franchetti)

Bells of Ireland (Molucella laevis)

Tansy (Tanacetum vulgare)

seed heads of *Clematis* and bittersweet
   (Celastrus)
shrubby hare's ear *(Bupleurum)*
smoke tree *(Cotinus)*
stonecrop *(Sedum)*
tansy *(Tanacetum vulgare)*
Teloxys aristata
wormwood *(Artemisia)*

Roses, peonies and ranunculus can also be air
dried. Stand the flowers in a vase to open, and
hang them up before they have opened fully.

Pearly everlasting (Helichrysum *'Schwefellicht'*, syn. Anaphalis
triplinervis *'Schwefellicht')*

Drying in the microwave or fan oven

There are also other methods. It is possible to
dry flowers in the microwave or fan oven. By
experimenting you can find out which flowers
lend themselves to this method and which do
not, and how long you need to leave particular
blooms in the oven.

Wiring various materials.

Drying with silica gel

Silica gel is another drying aid. Silica gel consists of hygroscopic crystals that you can buy from the chemist's. The granules are blue when they are dry and turn pink when they absorb moisture. They are quite large when you buy them however, and cannot be used in this form. Crush them in a mortar first. Some florists and garden centres sell special flower drying granules under various brand names.

The flowers you intend to dry should not have any moisture on them, since this will cause brown spots on the petals. To dry the flowers, place a thin layer of silica gel in the bottom of a box or biscuit tin. Leave on only a short length of stem. Make sure that the flowers are not touching one another. Carefully sprinkle silica gel or a proprietary flower drying product between the flowers until they are completely covered. By adding the drying agent layer by layer between the flowers you can keep an eye on the shape of the flower and take action if a petal is bent back. Tap the sides of the tin from time to time, or shake it gently, to ensure that the granules get right in among the petals; this is particularly important with double flowers. Once all the flowers are completely covered, put the lid on the tin. The length of time needed for the flowers to dry will depend on the species. This is why it is better to dry one type at a time. The drying process usually takes a

A wreath of dried flowers on a pewter plate.

Carthamus tinctorius

Statice (Limonium latifolium)

This wreath really brightens up the fence.

The wreath in shades of pink shows up well against the white wall.

few days to a week. Check from time to time to see how the drying process is going, since flowers left too long in silica gel become too brittle. When the gel granules have turned pink, you can assume they have done their job. Once the flowers have been gently removed from the granules (carefully tip off the top layer of granules), the discoloured granules can be dried for reuse by spreading them out on a baking sheet and placing them in a hot oven.

Drying with silver sand

Flowers can also be dried in dry silver sand. Because sand may sometimes appear dry when it actually isn't, and also to speed up the process, fine granules of silica gel can be added to the silver sand. Use two parts sand to one part silica gel. You can also use powdered alum or boracic acid powder instead of silica gel.

Drying special flowers
The previous two methods generally call for a great deal of time and patience, and afterwards each flower still has to be wired individually. It makes sense to keep this method for flowers that cannot be dried by air drying.
These include:

anemones
bellflowers
camellias
Christmas roses
narcissi
orchids
pompon dahlias
tulips
zinnias

Right: this Christmas wreath has a wonderful wintry quality.

A 'filled' wreath of dried flowers.

If you hang this wreath on your front door, every guest will feel welcome!

Below: the silver of the little baubles in the wreath is beautifully echoed in the four silver candles.

The golden baubles give this wreath a festive air.

Right: the combination of a dried flower wreath and a tall candle is very sophisticated.

This attractive display in pastel shades is arranged in florist's foam. A selection of dried flowers and grasses was used. Pale green hydrangeas (Hydrangea macrophylla) were pushed into the foam first, so that it was effectively concealed from view. They were followed by the delicate Helipterum manglesii in pink and white, white Gomphrena globosa, *carline thistles* (Carlina vulgaris), *quaking grass* (Briza minima) *and the flat seed heads of shepherd's purse* (Capsella bursa-pastoris).

Of course you can use dried flowers to create all sorts of lovely arrangements, but they can also simply be placed in bunches on top of a cupboard. An attractive decoration in the hall.

Below: an arrangement in an old fountain-just dried hydrangeas. These flowers have been arranged in dry florist's foam that was originally used for a display of fresh flowers.

A small, round arrangement in which the hydrangea flowers have been sprayed the same colour as the stemmed glass container. This creates a feeling of unity between the arrangement and the container. Tufts of lichen moss and larch cones have been added. The grey foliage and round flower heads come from an exotic plant. The shiny baubles add sparkle to this little display.

Drying with glycerine

Preparing flowers in glycerine generally produces a poor result, because the flowers become brown and greasy. This method is suitable for drying foliage. Since foliage is an extremely important factor in creating a good arrangement, you should give this method a try. You will achieve the best results if you preserve leaf-bearing branches of the brown beech,

Eucalyptus, Elaeagnus ebbingei, bay, laurel, ivy and hydrangea flowers (although these can also be air dried).

To preserve these materials, use two parts of

glycerine to three parts of hot water. Place the branches upright in about 10 cm (4 inches) of this mixture. Leave them like this in a cool place for about a week. When tiny drops of glycerine start appearing through the pores of the leaves, take the branches out of the mixture and rinse them off thoroughly.

Drying by pressing

Many people will be familiar with the technique of pressing flowers; most of us probably pressed flowers at school for a nature project or as a memento of a lovely holiday. Flowers and leaves you want to dry this way should not be too thick, not should they contain a lot of moisture. Whole flower spikes are usually not suitable either, since the spikes are very finely

A basket in grey and red. After Christmas you could perhaps replace the red additions with dried flowers so that the arrangement can continue to serve as a small decoration.

divided and are made up of very delicate florets. The flowers can be pressed between sheets

This arrangement has been created in a ball of florist's foam secured to the top of the glass candlestick. It consists of green hydrangea flowers, beech nuts (Fagus sylvatica), bay leaves (Laurus nobilis), oats (Avena sativa) and the white flowers of Helichrysum vestitum and Helipterum manglesii.

Various materials have been arranged in a cone of florist's foam. They include dyed hydrangea flowers, lichen moss, cypress cones (Cupressus macrocarpa), brown fake fruits and gold Christmas baubles.

Many exotic plants and flowers lend themselves to dried flower arrangements.

of blotting paper in a flower press, between books (but do bear in mind that the flowers can give off coloured sap), or between sheets of blotting paper under a heavy carpet or rug.

Place the flowers on the paper very carefully and flatten them slightly with your fingers, place another sheet of blotting paper on top and then a sheet of cardboard. For several layers in a flower press, put another sheet of blotting paper on the cardboard, flowers or leaves, more blotting paper and then another piece of cardboard. Pressed flowers cannot be used for three-dimensional arrangements, but they can look very pretty in a flat design on paper or fine fabric.

Wiring dried flowers

Their short stems mean that flowers dried in silica gel or silver sand have to be wired. Other dried flowers can sometimes also do with the support of a wire, since the stalks can become quite brittle after drying. Wiring flowers calls for some dexterity, particularly where small, delicate flowers are concerned. Use fine florist's wire or stub wire (0.4 mm) for these flowers. Slightly thicker wire (0.6 or 0.7 mm) is suitable for sturdier flowers.

The technique for wiring a single flower, a small clump of flowers and also ribbon is to take a stub wire and bend it more or less in the middle to create a large 'hairpin'. Pick up the

material you want to wire and the wire itself between the thumb and forefinger of one hand, holding them at the point where the wire is bent. The ends of the wire and the stems should be pointing in the same direction. With the other hand, wind one of the two wires around the other wire and the stems to secure them firmly. Strawflowers *(Helichrysum)* and sometimes also *Helipterum roseum* can be wired by pushing a wire up through the underside of the flower into the flower head, although not precisely in the centre. This wire should be bent into a hook first; this hook then ends up in the centre of the flower.

Leaves are wired by threading a wire (0.4 or 0.6 mm) through the back of the leaf, behind and at right angles to the main vein. Grasp the leaf at this point between thumb and forefinger. With your other hand, bend the two legs down

A Christmas ball arranged in a sphere of florist's foam. Lichen moss, larch cones, gold-painted hydrangea flowers and red and gold Christmas baubles are the ingredients. The brown, pointed, exotic-looking fruit is the base of a Protea flower head.

and wind one of them around the leaf stalk and the other leg.

Keeping dried flowers

Dried flowers will eventually lose their colour if they are exposed to light. The sunnier their position, the quicker they will fade.

It is consequently a good idea to store flowers you don't plan to use immediately-preferably in a box or tin-so that the flowers retain their colours and do not get dusty.

Christmas wreaths made from dried flowers should also be stored at the end of the festive season so that they can be used again the following year. Put the wreath between sheets of absorbent paper-newspaper will do-in a box with a well-fitting lid.

Wreaths

Magnificent wreaths can be made out of dried flowers, seed heads, various dried fruits and cones.
They can be hung up on the wall or door, but it can also be very effective to lay them on a

A subtle combination of white, grey, brown and silver.

Various bunches of dried flowers and grasses have been placed in a basket. Make sure you always have contrasts, because this will show off the individual materials to best effect. Start by positioning the materials with the longest stems-in this case the stalks with the fine seed heads of the flax plant (Linum usitatissimum), the blue thistles (Eryngium planum), the Helichrysum bracteatum) and the Gypsophila. On top of these lie little bunches of flowers, with the stems getting progressively shorter, such as the Helipterum, hydrangeas, another bunch of blue thistles and, in the foreground, the white pearly everlasting (Anaphalis triplinervis).

table, perhaps with candles in them. You can also place a dish on a foot or stand in the centre, holding fruit or a cake. Wreaths can also look very good with a candlestick placed in the centre.

If you use candles in association with dried flowers, be very conscious of the fire risk.

Detail of an arrangement containing hydrangeas, Eucalyptus, red roses and Helichrysum bracteatum. The oats (Avena sativa) add a lively touch.

You can easily make your own potpourri out of fragrant roses from the garden or roses used in an arrangement after they have faded. Dry the individual petals and add a few lavender flowers for extra scent.

Two magnificent flowers of the carline thistle (Carlina acaulis), showing their spiky bracts, arranged in a French flower basket. Never pick these thistles in the wild since they are on the list of protected species.

Below: red roses and pale green hydrangeas prevent this display, which is made up of a great many very delicate materials, from becoming too fussy.

A step-by-step guide

In this chapter, we take you step by step through the creation of some really lovely arrangements, illustrating each step with photographs.

Once you have mastered the technical aspects of flower arranging, you will soon find you can make a delightful bowl arrangement, a splendid Christmas decoration with elegant swags and garlands, and a magnificent wreath for the front door. Your personal choice of materials will give your creations a truly individual character.

Have a look in the florist's from time to time to get inspiration. Pictures and articles in magazines can also be helpful. The tools and equipment you need can be bought from any good garden centre and probably from your local florist's too.

Arrangement in a wire basket

1. Line a metal basket with a layer of sphagnum moss and cover it with a good-sized piece of plastic sheeting. Place several blocks of well-soaked florist's foam in the basket and fill any spaces between the plastic and the basket with more sphagnum moss so that the plastic and the foam are concealed when viewed from the side.

2. Once the sphagnum moss has been pressed down well all round, you can cut off any excess plastic sticking up above the edge of the basket. Push a stick into the florist's foam in the middle of the basket. This is to help in making the arrangement and will be removed later.

3. Now push the foliage (Gaultheria shallon) and the fern fronds into the florist's foam. Do this in such a way that they are all pointing towards the centre and towards the bottom of the stick. Always arrange bent stems so that they curve over the edge of the basket and the upper surface of the leaves is visible.

4. After the foliage come the flowers. Start by putting the round, relatively compact flowers (in this case the scabious) in the centre. Turn the basket regularly so that the flowers are evenly spaced. Next to go in are the Ageratums and the delphiniums. The small asters go in next and can stand out slightly. And finally the Veronica spikes are used to fill in any gaps.

Small round arrangement in a glass vase

2. *Start by arranging a basis of leaves in the florist's foam-in this case ivy and Skimmia. Because the foam protrudes above the edge of the vase, you can put leaves and twigs in almost horizontally so that they hang down over the edge of the container and conceal the bottom of the foam.*

4. *Now the flowers go in —first the large trumpet-shaped* Lavatera, *which are pushed well in, and then the annual delphiniums* (Delphinium grandiflorum), *which stand out above them. The last to go in are the spikes of gardener's garters* (Phalaris canariensis).

1. *In a transparent container, you do not want to see the arranging materials, such as florist's foam, pin-holders or chicken wire. The florist's foam in this stemmed glass vase is placed so that it is in the top of the vase only. The two wooden skewers pushed through the foam at right angles and balanced on the edge of the vase will keep the foam from sinking.*

3. *Next comes the green Bupleurum. This annual has a very bushy habit, which means that a single stem will have lots of side shoots that can be used individually in a small arrangement. Turn the vase regularly to make sure that you are maintaining the round shape.*